Demolition

By Anne O'Brien

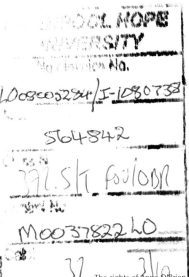
Series Literacy Consultant
Dr Ros Fisher

PEARSON
Longman

Pearson Education Limited
Edinburgh Gate
Harlow
Essex CM20 2JE
England

www.longman.co.uk

ISBN 0 582 84123 2

Colour reproduction by Colourscan, Singapore
Printed and bound in China by Leo Paper Products Ltd.

The Publisher's policy is to use paper manufactured from sustainable forests.

10 9 8 7 6 5 4 3

The following people from **DK** have
contributed to the development of this product:
Art Director Rachael Foster

Martin Wilson **Mangaing Art Editor**	**Managing Editor** Marie Greenwood
Emy Manby **Design**	**Editorial** Hannah Wilson
Helen McFarland **Picture Research**	**Production** Gordana Simakovic
Richard Czapnik, Andy Smith **Cover Design**	**DTP** David McDonald

Consultant Howard Button

Dorling Kindersley would like to thank: Brent Blanchard at Implosionworld; National Federation of Demolition Contractors, UK; Lucy Heaver for editorial research; Rose Horridge in the DK Picture Library; Ed Merrit for cartography; Kath Northam for additional design work; Johnny Pau for additional cover design work; and Barry Poskanzer.

Picture Credits: Alamy Images: Tim Keatley 11r. Associated Press AP: Lennox McLendon 20br. Construction Photography.com: Jean-Francois Cardella 13; Paul McMullin 7br; Rae Cooper 1, 5tr, 9tr, 12–13b, 30–31. Corbis: Nathan Benn 23br; Bettmann 24; Caron (NPP) Philippe/Sygma 4–5; DiMaggio/Kalish 28–29; Chinch Gryniewicz/Ecoscene 3; Colin Garratt 11cl; Hans Halberstadt 26–27; Dave G. Houser 25; Otto Lang 5cr, 22b; Durand Patrick/SYGMA 7tr; Chris Rainier 23tr; Roger Ressmeyer 8–9, Sorbo Robert/Sygma 16–17, 18bl, 18br, 19bl, 19br; David Turnley 10tr; Peter Turnley 4tr; Stewart Tilger 26bc. Getty Images: AFP 14–15; David Boyer/National Geographic Image Collection 23tl. Implosion World: 13cr, 18tr, 21br, 30cl, 31tr. Reuters: Aaron Mayes 20r; Peter Macdairmid/PKM 15tr; STR 19tr. Science Photo Library: Pascal Goetgheluck 13br; Heini Schneebeli 29br; Charles D. Winters 17cr. Cover: Getty Images: Fred Charles front t. Rex Features: DCY front br.

All other images: DK Dorling Kindersley © 2004. For further information see www.dkimages.com
Dorling Kindersley Ltd., 80 Strand, London WC2R ORL

CONTENTS

WHAT IS DEMOLITION?

Demolition means the taking down of a building or other structure, usually by destroying it.

Some buildings must be demolished because they are old and falling apart, and they cannot be repaired. Natural disasters, such as fires, floods or earthquakes also damage buildings, making them unsafe. At other times, an older building needs to be removed to make room for something new.

The people of Berlin reunited their city by demolishing the Berlin Wall. Much of the demolition was done by hand.

Three Types of Demolition

Different buildings need different methods of demolition. There are three main types of demolition:

- **Mechanical demolition** uses machines to topple, cut and crush parts of buildings.
- **Explosive demolition** uses controlled blasts to cause a building to topple or to implode (collapse inwards).
- **Dismantling demolition** is the careful salvage, or rescue, of structures that are often historically or culturally important.

mechanical demolition

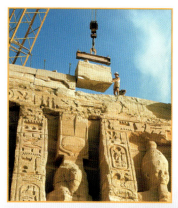

dismantling demolition

These buildings in France are being destroyed by explosive demolition.

Understanding Structures

Buildings are built to be sturdy and stable. In certain places they have to withstand hurricanes and earthquakes. This can make them difficult to demolish.

Before a demolition project starts, the demolition company has to understand how a structure was built. They must know if the building is made of wood, metal, steel-reinforced concrete or other materials. Then they can choose the right materials for the job and work out how much of the building can be recycled. Sometimes the contractor who constructed the building provides this information.

wood

metal (steel girder)

steel-reinforced concrete

Pyramids

A few thousand years ago, very tall structures had to have a wide base. Without a wide base to support it, the structure would be unstable and could topple over. The largest of the ancient Egyptian pyramids, the Great Pyramid, has a base that is more than 228 metres wide. This enabled it to be built more than 146 metres high.

Egypt's Great Pyramid

The ancient Egyptians used stone to build their pyramids.

Planning and Safety

Demolition is dangerous. It is very important to keep workers, the public and the environment safe. For example, the contractor must be aware of any hazardous materials in a building, such as lead or asbestos. By law, these materials must be carefully removed and disposed of safely.

From a safe distance away, a demolition expert closely watches a controlled explosion. He uses a radio to talk to the rest of the demolition team.

Demolition companies work with many different groups to ensure safety. Building owners, architects, engineers and council workers all play a role. Contractors often work with the police, especially if a project is in a crowded area.

Demolition contractors discuss every detail before taking a structure down.

! Do not enter demolition or building sites. They are dangerous areas, often containing unstable structures, heavy machinery and hazardous materials.

MECHANICAL DEMOLITION

Demolishing buildings with explosives is dramatic, but rare. In most demolition projects, machines topple, cut or crush the materials of a building. Common types of equipment used for mechanical demolition include the wrecking ball, the excavator and the digger, or front-end loader.

Mechanical demolition is often cheaper, safer and easier to manage than explosive demolition. It takes longer to carry out a demolition with machines, but it requires less preparation and security. However, it is just as important to work safely.

Gravity

Demolition takes advantage of gravity. The pull of the Earth's gravity causes all matter to move towards Earth's centre. A building's structural supports prevent floors and walls from collapsing. Demolition aims to remove those supports to let gravity bring a building tumbling down.

Tools for the Project

The oldest and most frequently used large demolition tool is the wrecking ball. It is useful for smashing walls that are more than four storeys high because the ball hangs from a tall crane.

A digger may move in next to push over lower sections of the building. Then an excavator might cut out sections of the structure or break walls into small pieces. Finally a digger scoops up debris for recycling and disposal. Sorting may occur on site or elsewhere. A detailed plan for the demolition project indicates which of these tools and machines will be used and in what order.

A crane and wrecking ball demolish a building.

A digger removes rubble from the demolition site.

An excavator may also scoop up debris.

Toppling

A wrecking ball can also be used to destroy a whole building. A typical ball weighs about 2.2 tonnes and hangs from a tall crane by a cable. The continuous action of the heavy swinging ball knocking into a structure breaks the building apart.

It takes great skill to use a wrecking ball. The operator calculates exactly how far back to move the crane's long arm, called the "boom", and how far to let out the cable holding the ball. He or she needs to know when to release the ball so that it will swing towards the building at the right point and with just the right force. The operator must also plan the arc of the swing so the ball doesn't hit the crane when it swings back.

wrecking ball

Pendulums

A wrecking ball works like a pendulum. It is a weight hanging from a fixed point. When the weight is pulled off-centre in one direction and released, it swings through the centre to the opposite side. Gravity pulls it back towards the centre of the swing. Then the ball's momentum, or movement, carries it through that centre and almost back to its initial position.

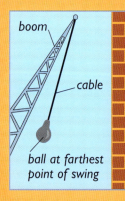

boom

cable

ball at farthest point of swing

At the point farthest from the building, the ball contains potential energy – energy that is stored when an object is on the brink of movement.

ball in motion

As the ball swings towards the building, its potential energy becomes kinetic energy – the energy of motion. This kinetic energy knocks into the wall with great force.

Lifting

Cranes have other jobs in demolition, too. Large pieces of a building can be grabbed and lifted by a crane with a grappling hook. This equipment was used for some of the Berlin Wall demolition. Sections of the wall were constructed of linked slabs of concrete. Cranes lifted out whole sections at a time.

This crane is grabbing scrap metal with its huge grappling hook.

grappling hook

Cutting, Crushing and Pounding

Another machine often used in demolition is the excavator, which can weigh between 7 and 90 tonnes. An excavator looks similar to a crane, but has a long computer-controlled arm at one end.

An excavator's strength comes from its use of fluid under pressure. This pressure, called hydraulic pressure, allows the machine to exert great force.

Hydraulics

Many demolition devices use hydraulics. A hydraulic device uses fluid contained in a sealed tube called a cylinder. The cylinder has a piston inside that applies pressure to the fluid. The cylinder is connected to a second and larger cylinder. A small amount of force applied to the fluid in the smaller cylinder will produce a much greater pushing force in the larger cylinder.

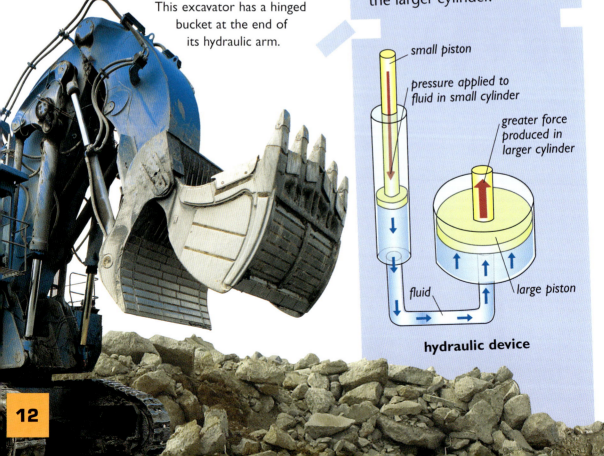

This excavator has a hinged bucket at the end of its hydraulic arm.

small piston

pressure applied to fluid in small cylinder

greater force produced in larger cylinder

fluid

large piston

hydraulic device

An excavator's arm can have a number of different attachments that either pull down a structure or grab, cut, crush or push debris. Shears can be attached to an excavator's arm to cut through steel and concrete like scissors cut through paper. Grapples, also called claw buckets, have metal teeth to bite out a section of wall or grab hold of a support and pull. Hydraulic hammer attachments, called breakers, pound and smash. Crushers grasp concrete chunks in their powerful jaws and crush them with metal teeth.

breaker

shears

Hydrodemolition

In hydrodemolition, jets of high-pressure water, often mixed with sand, scour away concrete and leave materials such as steel undamaged. It is a cleaner, safer and quieter alternative to the pneumatic drill.

concrete crusher

A technician uses a hydrodemolition machine to remove damaged concrete.

WEMBLEY STADIUM

Wembley Stadium was built in London in 1923. In 1948
the Olympics were held there. In 1966 the World Cup
was also held at Wembley, and England beat Germany
in the final.

Some years later, plans were made to build a bigger
stadium that would seat up to 90,000 people.

In summer 2002 demolition began. Wembley Stadium
was most famous for its two 35-metre-high towers. These
became the first two targets for the demolition team.

The demolition of Wembley
took about five months.

On 7th December 2002 the concrete crowns of the towers, which had stood for seventy-nine years, were taken down in twenty minutes. Parts of the crowns were saved for reuse. Two months later a giant excavator began removing the rest of the towers from the top down. Bulldozers also worked to remove other sections of the stadium. Ceramic tiles commemorating the 1948 Olympics were carefully removed from the stadium's walls and preserved.

The huge excavator that demolished Wembley's famous towers was given the name *Goliath*.

EXPLOSIVE DEMOLITION

Explosive demolition is the destruction of a building by the use of controlled blasting. The blasting weakens a building's supports so that the walls collapse inwards. This effect is called an implosion, even though the process that causes it is a series of explosions.

Explosive demolition is used in special cases. Some buildings are too tall to be torn down by machine. Others are so close to neighbouring structures that there is no room for demolition machinery to move. When a building or other structure is very tall, explosive demolition is the safest, and sometimes cheapest, option.

The twenty-four-year-old Kingdome, a stadium in Seattle, Washington, USA, was explosively demolished in March 2000 to make way for a new stadium.

Implosion

In demolition terms, "implosion" describes the way a structure collapses inwards, leaving a pile of rubble in the area that the building once occupied. An implosion is often used in tightly packed areas to demolish a structure without damaging nearby buildings. Explosives are carefully set up to cause the building to implode, or collapse in upon itself.

sides of building fall inwards

A building implodes.

Blasters

The planning process for an explosive demolition is even more detailed than for a demolition using machines. An explosive-demolition expert, or blaster, has to consider many things. How tall is the building? What area does it occupy? How will the blast affect nearby buildings? The challenge is to find the best way to get a building to fall down safely.

Dynamite

Alfred Nobel invented dynamite in 1866. It was used during World War I and World War II by soldiers to destroy bridges, factories and railways. Soldiers then used their experience to become the first demolition experts in the building industry. Dynamite is still used in demolition today.

sticks of dynamite

17

A Matter of Timing

After careful planning, a deconstruction crew gets to work. They weaken the building using drills, pneumatic drills and welding torches. They cut supports, punch holes and knock down walls so that the building will come down easily with a minimum of explosives.

Then the blasters attach the explosives, which have built-in timing devices, to every concrete post or steel beam on the first few floors. To prevent chunks of concrete from flying out, workers may cover the concrete posts. The explosives themselves are also wrapped to make sure the timing devices and the charges are not disturbed until it is their turn to blast. Even nearby buildings may be wrapped in tough fabric to protect them from flying debris.

This blaster is operating a hand-held seismograph, an instrument that records shock waves produced by earthquakes or demolitions.

The Kingdome demolition begins.

A few seconds later, there are more explosions.

18

On the day of the blast, the team checks each switch and wire. The wires connect the explosives to a command post, a safe distance away. The demolition team gathers at the command post to set off the explosions. As the time for the blast nears, a siren warns of the coming explosion. One minute later the push of a button activates the explosives.

The explosives don't all go off at once, but in a sequence that helps the building collapse as planned. Often the lower floors or base of a structure are exploded first so that upper sections collapse of their own accord. Timing devices also ensure that the building falls in the safest direction. An enormous building, which may have taken many years to build, comes down in just a few seconds.

A few days before the demolition of the Kingdome, a demolition expert shows the media the device that will be used to trigger the implosion.

The series of explosions continues.

Twenty seconds later, only rubble remains.

LANDMARK HOTEL

Las Vegas, Nevada, in the United States has been the site of a number of building implosions, as old hotels and casinos are frequently demolished to make way for new ones. In November 1995 the 111-metre-high Landmark Hotel was demolished. At that time, the hotel was the second largest building ever imploded. (The largest was in Brazil.)

This explosive demolition promised to be so spectacular that film-makers decided to make it part of a science-fiction film called *Mars Attacks!* The director of the film contacted the demolition company and made arrangements to film the demolition. This dramatic film footage eventually found its way onto the big screen.

Landmark Hotel before demolition

Carefully positioned dynamite brought down the west side of the hotel first.

STELCO STEEL PLANT

The 1997 demolition of the Stelco Steel Plant in Ontario, Canada, jointly holds the world record for the most structures demolished at one time. When the plant was demolished, twenty buildings were taken down at once. These included storage sheds, warehouses and smokestacks.

The buildings were made of steel, not of concrete. Structural steel is much denser, stronger and more flexible than concrete. A high-powered explosive called RDX had to be used to slice through the steel supports. In some cases, the steel columns had to be cut mechanically before they could be demolished.

Smokestacks at Stelco were toppled by explosive demolition.

21

DISMANTLING DEMOLITION

Most demolition involves toppling, cutting, crushing or blasting. Sometimes, though, the purpose of a demolition is not to get rid of a structure but to save it. Saving a structure is often difficult work because every part of the building must be protected as it is dismantled. Then the structure can be put back together in another place.

Abu Simbel is a set of two ancient Egyptian temples that were carefully dismantled from the original site where they had been built more than 3,000 years ago. The temples, which include four 20-metre-high statues of Pharaoh Rameses II, were in danger of being washed away by Lake Nasser on the River Nile.

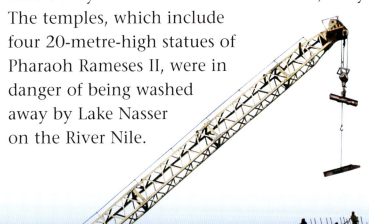

The Abu Simbel temples were cut out of the rock from which they had been carved and lifted up the cliff by cranes.

original site of Abu Simbel

current site of Abu Simbel

From 1964 to 1968 the temples and their statues were carefully dismantled, moved farther up the cliff and reassembled. An artificial mountain was built behind the temples to match the original cliffs from which the temples had been carved.

Ancient Egyptian temples are not the only structures to be rebuilt. Almost 200 years ago, Native American people called the Oneida built log cabins in present-day Wisconsin, USA. Over time, the Oneida people built more modern buildings and stopped using the log cabins. In the 1990s, five of the cabins were carefully taken apart and stored. Every log was marked so that the cabins could be rebuilt in their original form. Recently the cabins were reassembled to become part of a living history exhibition in a historical park in Wisconsin.

Originally, the Oneida lived in longhouses: pole frames covered with tree bark. This is a reconstructed longhouse.

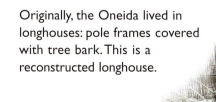

LONDON BRIDGE

In 1962 London Bridge was sinking into the soft mud of the River Thames in London. A new bridge was needed.

A wealthy businessman called Robert McCulloch offered to buy the old bridge. He wanted to take it apart and ship it to the United States. He planned to reassemble it in Lake Havasu City, Arizona. Everyone thought he was foolish. Why would anyone want to put a 140-year-old bridge in the desert of Arizona?

London Bridge originally spanned the River Thames in London.

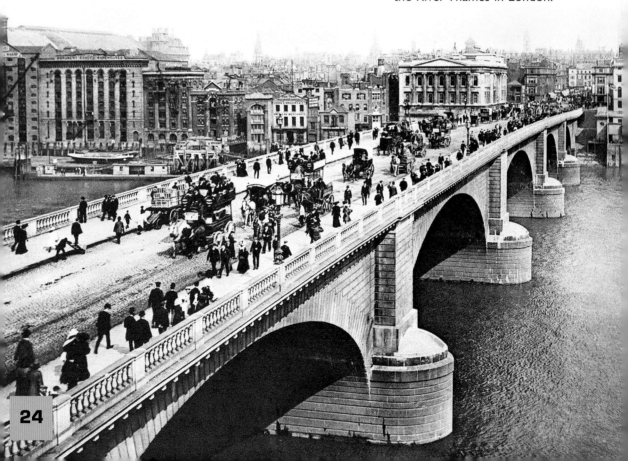

However, McCulloch was serious. He bought the bridge for $2.5 million (£1 million) in 1968. It took three years to break the bridge into 10,276 pieces. These pieces were then flown to the United States, driven to the Arizona site and reconstructed. The bridge was put up over a specially dug channel that lead to an artificially made lake called Lake Havasu.

Over the years, the bridge project has become a tourist attraction. Today London Bridge is one of Arizona's favourite tourist spots. A unique piece of architecture has been saved, too.

Since 1971 London Bridge has stood near Lake Havasu in Arizona.

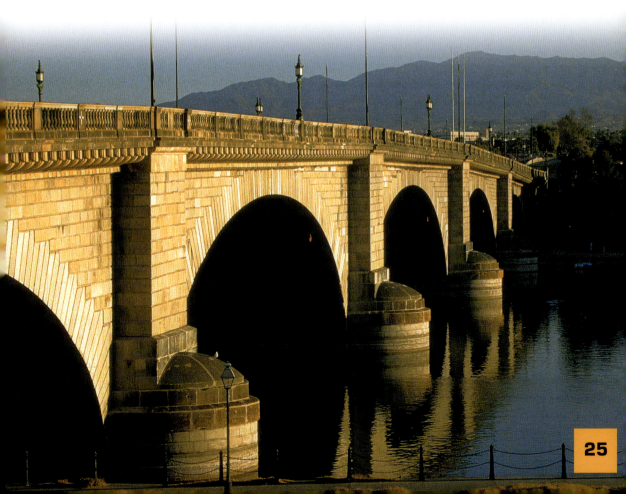

CLEAN-UP AND SALVAGE

Tearing a building down is one challenge. Cleaning up afterwards is another. No matter how a building is demolished, the result is the same. An enormous pile of rubble has to be sorted and removed. Some of the debris, such as good-quality brick and steel, is recycled. Some is discarded. The demolition job isn't complete until the site is clean.

bulldozer with caterpillar tracks

Bulldozers and diggers help with the clean-up. The bulldozer's wide, flat blade shovels large amounts of material into piles. It can clear wide areas and move heavy loads because of its pushing strength.

Caterpillar Tracks

Vehicles with wheels and rubber tyres are faster than those with tank-like tracks, but the uneven ground of a demolition site makes the tank-tread design more effective. The track rolls over the rough surface of the debris, crushing it under its weight. The track also distributes the weight of heavy machinery more evenly over rough ground, making equipment less likely to overturn.

Tank-tread tracks move easily over uneven ground.

World's Largest Dustpan

A digger, or front-end loader, works like a dustpan, scooping up rubble into its bucket. First the digger is driven to a pile, and its bucket is dropped. Then the operator rotates the bucket which forces rubble into it. Next the operator lifts the bucket high above the digger into the carrying position so that none of the rubble can fall out. Finally the digger is driven to the site's "target", the pile or the container where the debris is dumped. A skilled digger operator can do this sequence more than one hundred times in an hour. A dumper truck often removes the debris from the site.

dumper truck

A digger empties rubble from a demolition site.

Recycling

Many materials used to build a structure can be recycled. Some materials are removed before a building is demolished. Other materials are collected afterwards. Demolition companies recycle steel beams, reinforced bars, pipe, copper wire, good brick, sheets of aluminium and even panels of dried plaster called drywall. A big part of demolition work is sorting through these materials. Those that can be recycled must be separated from those that can't. Sometimes an excavator is used to sort material.

Hand-made bricks, ironwork and even sinks are carefully salvaged from buildings and resold.

Some materials can't be recycled. Shattered bricks and wood scraps go to landfill sites. The digger crushes this debris so it fits more compactly into the dumper trucks that carry it away.

An excavator sorts through huge piles of scrap metal.

Saving Money and Materials

The steel or iron parts in buildings are often salvaged and recycled. Recycling is done for many reasons. Demolition contractors would rather receive money for salvaged materials than pay money to landfill operators for the rubble they have to dump.

Some concrete and brick can be crushed and recycled to make new concrete. One Australian company uses an on-site crusher mounted on tracks. During one project in Sydney, for example, this crusher recycled 30,000 tonnes of concrete. Crushed concrete can be mixed and used for roads and building foundations. Recycling materials also helps the environment because it reduces the number of landfill sites needed.

Recycling Steel

Less energy and fewer raw materials are needed to recycle old steel than to make new steel. Recycled steel, therefore, is less expensive and more environmentally friendly. Making new steel requires a blast furnace, iron ore, coke and limestone. Because of the extreme heat and time required, blast furnaces use a lot of energy. Recycled scrap steel is remelted in an electric furnace which uses less energy than a blast furnace.

Electric furnaces melt scrap steel to make recycled steel.

CONCLUSION

Demolition is a destructive, yet delicate, process. Contractors must plan every last detail of timing and tools before they begin to tear down a building. They must take into consideration how the building was constructed, what its surrounding area is like, which type of demolition they will use and how they will remove the huge pile of rubble that is left. A few explosions may bring a building down in seconds, but the whole process of demolition is long and painstaking.

The Bow Valley Medical Centre, in Calgary, Canada, and the Stelco Steel plant jointly hold the record for the most buildings demolished at once.

The longest structure ever demolished with explosives was a bridge in Ohio. The 817-metre-long bridge was demolished in November 2003.

Demolition changes the look of our urban and rural landscapes.

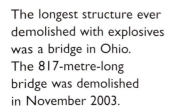

Demolition contractors have been called upon to take down all kinds of structures. These include stadiums, department stores, factories, hotels and towers. Communities will always be looking for ways to reuse valuable space and materials. The skills and equipment of demolition workers will continue to be in demand and, as a result, our architectural landscape will constantly be changing.

INDEX

564842